Mind Tricks

Peter Eldin

Copper Beech Books
Brookfield, Connecticut

© Aladdin Books Ltd 2002
Produced by
Aladdin Books Ltd
28 Percy Street
London W1T 2BZ

ISBN 0–7613–2824–6

First published in the United States in 2002 by
Copper Beech Books,
an imprint of
The Millbrook Press
2 Old New Milford Road
Brookfield, Connecticut 06804

Designers:
Flick, Book Design & Graphics
Pete Bennett

Editor:
Leen De Ridder

Illustrators:
Catherine Ward – SGA
Ian Thompson

Cataloging-in-Publication data
is on file at the Library of Congress

Photo Credits:
Abbreviations: l-left, r-right-top, b-bottom, c-center, m-middle
All photos by Select Pictures, except:
15br – The Edwin A. Dawes Collection.
Picture research by Brian Hunter Smart

10 9 8 7 6 5 4 3 2 1

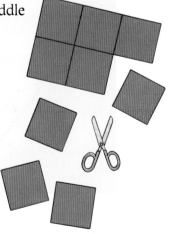

Contents

⭐ 4 Introduction
How to use this book

⭐ 6 Find the lady
Find one girl among eight boys

⭐ 8 Special sticks
Tell what happened while your back was turned

⭐ 10 Calculated in advance
Predict what number the audience writes down

⭐ 12 Dotty deception
A spectator throws two dice; you can tell what the numbers are

⭐ 14 What's the word?
You know what word—from an entire dictionary—was picked!

⭐ 16 A number in mind
Read someone's mind!

⭐ 18 Animal magic
There is a lion in the room!

⭐ 20 It's in the stars
Find the odd one out in a number of cards

⭐ 22 Divide by four
Make a very long number divisible by four

⭐ 24 Pick a book
You can tell which book was picked

⭐ 26 Odd and even
With your X-ray vision you can see what is hidden in a spectator's closed hands

⭐ 28 Reds and blacks
Predict how a deck of cards will be dealt

⭐ 30 Symbols of magic
Identify the symbol someone is thinking of

⭐ 32 Index and glossary
What magic words mean and where to find magic clubs and Web sites

Introduction

Magic, the art of doing things contrary to the laws of nature, appeals to people all over the world. Magic is a great hobby and will let you amaze and entertain your family and friends! In *Mind Tricks*, you can learn how to read your friends' minds and even how to predict the future!

How to learn tricks

1. Read through the whole trick twice. Don't worry if you do not understand everything at this stage.

2. Gather all the things you need.

3. Go through the trick again, doing the actions step by step.

4. If you are not comfortable with a particular action, see if you can adapt it to suit you better.

5. Now practice the various movements, making sure that your hands are in the right place and that you can move smoothly from one step to another.

6. Once you have practiced the moves, you can start rehearsing the trick (performing it as if for a real audience).

7. When you are sure that you can perform the trick perfectly, try it out on your friends.

Top Tip

Watch for this symbol to read some top tips! They will help you make more of a trick or give you useful extra information.

Magicians and their magic
In boxes like this one, you will find information about famous magicians and their tricks.

IT'S **mAGIc**

4

HINTS

• Never repeat a trick in the same company. The first showing of a trick amazes the audience. Do it again and they will know what is coming. The element of surprise will have gone and the trick will not go down as well. Because they know what is coming the second time around, it is also easier for the audience to figure out how the trick is done.

• Your success as a magician will depend a lot on the way you present a trick. Even the simplest trick can look fantastic if you perform it confidently and without hesitating. This may sound like a strange piece of advice, but your performance of magic will improve if you believe that what you are doing really is magic. Believe you are doing real magic and you will be!

• When people ask how your tricks are done, do not tell them. Although many people may ask, they will be disappointed when you let them know how simple some tricks really are. Keep the secrets secret!

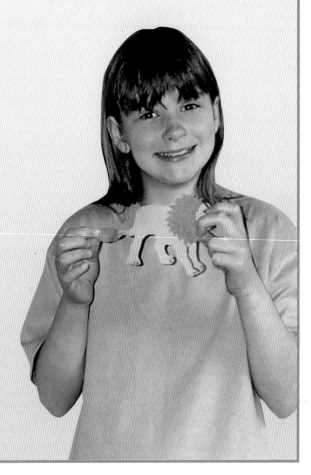

These exclamation marks tell you what to look for in certain tricks or in the preparation for them. They may look like unimportant details when you first read them, but you may give away the trick if you ignore them.

Find the lady

THE TRICK

Eight boys' names and one girl's name are written down. You are able to pick out the girl's name with your eyes shut!

Preparation

You will need:
• a big piece of thin cardboard
• pens or pencils
• a paper bag or a box

Tear the cardboard into nine equal rectangles.

Hand the rectangles out to the spectators and ask eight of them to write down a boy's name. Ask the ninth spectator to write the name of a girl. Make sure this is the person who got the center rectangle.

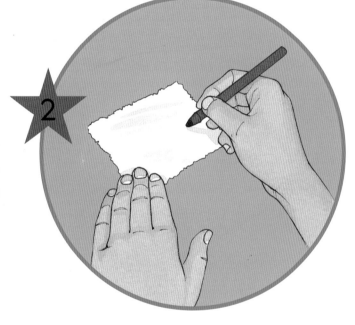

Artistic mind

Karl Germain (1878-1959) was famous for the elegant way he presented his tricks. He brought this same artistry to the performance of mind magic. In one of his mind reading tricks he drew on a blackboard a picture that a spectator was merely thinking of. He also performed a thought reading act with an assistant using a secret code based on the Morse code. He retired from the stage in 1911 to study law.

IT'S **MAGIC**

3

When all the cards are in the paper bag or box, mix them up. Now shut your eyes and reach into the bag. Run your finger over the cards and you will be able to feel the difference between the girl's name and the others. This is because the center rectangle has four rough edges (as you can see in Step 1). All the other rectangles have at least one smooth edge.

4

Take out the girl's name card, read out the name, and take your bow.

Top Tip

You can make this trick appear even more impressive by using a blindfold. Ask one spectator to tie it around your head and another to confirm that you can't see anything. Then ask someone to guide you back to the box or bag to take out the card.

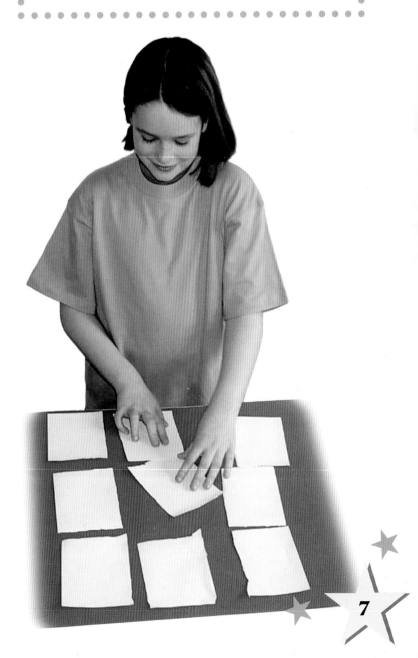

Special sticks

THE TRICK

You tell the audience how many popsicle sticks they have moved...while your back was turned!

Preparation

You will need:
- 13 popsicle sticks (or coffee stirrers)

Mark the sticks from 0 to 12. You can mark them either with numbers or dots—a bit like dominoes—to make them look more magical. You could also devise your own secret symbol system. Just make sure you remember which symbol stands for which number!

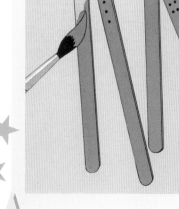

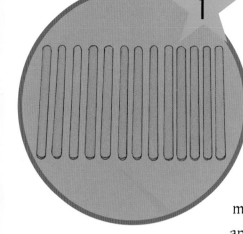

1 Arrange the sticks in a row, with 0 at the left and 12 at the right with the numbers face down. The blank sides must be face up. Tell the audience a magic story about how you got these sticks made of a special kind of wood on your travels. You have learned from an old and wise magician how to read the sticks and tell if any have been moved.

Say that you want any small number of sticks moved while your back is turned. You show how to do this by moving one stick at a time from the left end to the right end. Let's say you move three sticks.

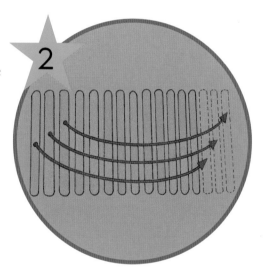

2

Top Tip

- *You can also do this trick with dominoes or pieces of paper instead of coffee stirrers.*
- *You could use more than 13 of them, as long as you keep a '0' at the lefthand side of the row. The trick will still work, and the more sticks or other objects you have, the more sticks your audience can move, and the more spectacular your mental powers will appear!*

8

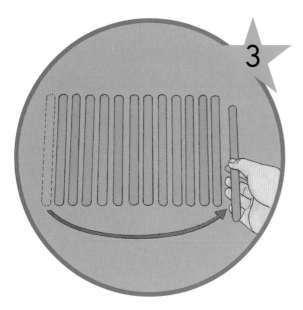

3

Turn your back and ask the spectator to move any small number of sticks from the left end to the right end. Let's say he moves six sticks.

Turn around again and mentally counting from the right end the number of sticks you had moved (three in our example), lift the last stick and this will indicate how many sticks have been moved. In the picture, the third stick from the right has six spots, which means that the spectator has moved six sticks.

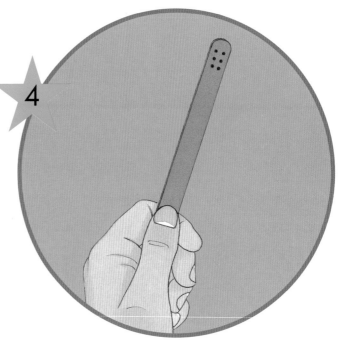

4

Calculated in advance

THE TRICK

Predict the sum of numbers that spectators write down randomly.

Preparation

You will need:
- a notepad
- a pen or pencil
- the ability to do some mental arithmetic

1 Write a number on the pad, tear off the sheet, and fold it up. Don't show it to the audience. This is your prediction. As an example, let us say you have written 42.

For my next trick...
In May 2002, David Blaine, America's best-known illusionist, emerged safely from a stack of boxes after a death defying leap, having spent just under 35 hours on a 22-in circular platform 80 ft high in New York City. Next, the modern-day Houdini is to be chained and thrown off Tower Bridge into the Thames River in England.

IT'S **mAGIc**

2 Take the pad to one of the spectators and ask her to write any number from 1 to 9 on the pad. Then go to several other spectators and ask them to do the same, writing their number below the previous one each time. While you are doing this, you are secretly adding up the numbers in your head.

3

Top Tip

The larger the number you put on your prediction paper, the more impressive the trick. But remember it is also harder for you to add up all the numbers in your head!

When the total comes within nine of your predicted number, take the notepad. Ask the last spectator for his name and make a show of writing it below the column of figures. But first, write the number that will bring the total to the number in your prediction.

4

Hand the pad to the spectator whose name you wrote down, and ask him to add up all the numbers and call out the total. If your mental arithmetic is correct, the total will be 42 (or whatever number you predicted). Get someone to open out the paper to show that your incredible power helped you predict what would happen.

11

Dotty deception

THE TRICK

A spectator throws two dice while your back is turned. With a simple calculation, you can tell what numbers the spectator threw. Spooky!

Preparation

You will need:
• colored cardboard
• a marker pen
• scissors
• two dice
• a notepad and pen

1 Cut a strip of cardboard and write numbers 1 to 6 on it.
2 Cut a second strip of cardboard twice as wide as the number strip and half as long.
3 Cut a hole in one of its sides large enough to show one number on the number strip.
4 Fold the strip lengthwise and tape it together to make a sleeve.
5 Slip the strip with the numbers into the sleeve. You will use this "number display" to show the numbers you choose.

Ask someone to throw the two dice on the table while your back is turned. As him to hide the dice. Let's say he threw a 4 and a 6.

Give him the pen and notepad to do some calculations. Ask him to double the first number thrown, add 5 then multiply the total by 5.

Finally, ask him to add the number on the second die to the total. (In our example: 65 + 6 = 71)

**71 – 25
= 46**

Ask him to read his final total. In your head, subtract 25 from the total. The result will be a two-figure number—the numbers of the two dice! In our example, 71 – 25 = 46. The spectator threw a 4 and a 6.

Now turn back to the audience and take your number display. Ask the spectator to think very hard of the number of the first die. Slowly slide the numbers back and forth and stop, for our example, at number 4. Then do the same for the other number. You can slide past the correct number a couple of times to keep up the suspense. Congratulate your spectator on his powerful mind, and take a bow!

Top Tip

- *If you are not sure if your spectator will add up his numbers correctly, you can either ask someone else to check his calculations or you can give him a calculator.*
- *You can invent a story about the number sleeve you use to get your audience's attention and make the trick appear more magical.*

What's the word?

THE TRICK

Read someone's mind and "see" what word they are looking at in a dictionary.

Preparation

You will need:
- two identical dictionaries
- cardboard
- scissors
- glue
- a marker pen
- a magic wand

1 Put one dictionary in the room where you are going to do the trick and hide the other one in the next room.

2 Cut out 26 cards and write the letters of the alphabet on them. (1 card for each letter).

3 Glue the letter cards to a big piece of cardboard.

Hand the dictionary to a spectator and ask someone else to call out any page number. Ask the person holding the book to look at the chosen page and read the word at the top, but not yet say it.

Now ask your spectator to show the word to the rest of the audience while you go into the next room. Close the door and quickly get the book you hid earlier. Turn to the chosen page number and memorize the word at the top of the page.

Top Tip

If you don't have two identical dictionaries to do this book test, you could borrow a schoolbook from a classmate—make sure it is exactly the same version as the one you have—and use that instead. Be aware that your classmate might know what is going on if he watches you do the trick. Either let him in on your secret, or make sure he is not there when you do the trick.

Hide the
book again
and then go back
into the room where everyone is waiting. Ask the spectator
with the dictionary to think of the word. Give him the
magic wand and ask him to "send" the word to the wand.
Then take your magic wand and slowly
spell out the word you have memorized,
letting the wand "guide" you to the correct
letters. It is of course the word he was
thinking of!

America's great mind reader
*In the 1940s, many were
convinced that American
Joseph Dunninger (1892-1975;
below at left) could read
minds. In his popular radio
and TV shows and personal
appearances, he would tell
people their innermost
thoughts. On one occasion the
description of someone was
written down and kept secret
by a committee of people.
From a crowd of 3,000
people, Dunninger found the
person described.*

15

A number in mind

THE TRICK

A spectator writes down a number and shows it to the audience without you seeing it. You then read a spectator's mind and say what number it was.

Preparation

You will need:
- paper
- a pen or pencil

You will need to do some secret practicing with a friend.

Ask someone to write down any three-digit number but not to let you see it. Ask him to show it to the audience.

Top Tip

When you practice with your friend, try to find out what the least obvious way of tightening and loosening her jaw is. You will be able to feel even a small jaw movement at your friend's temples. It is a good idea to practice in front of a mirror, so you can be sure that the expression on your friend's face does not show that she is involved in the trick. She should appear to be surprised that you are able to read her mind by putting your hand on her temples. At the end of the trick, when you reveal the number, your friend should appear impressed.

Then go to the friend you practiced with beforehand and place your hands on her temples.

3

Your friend tightens and loosens her jaw several times to signal each digit, leaving a slight pause between each so you can tell which is which. You will be able to feel the muscle movements and can then tell everyone what the chosen number was.

IT'S mAGIc

Minds in contact

The first mind reader to make great use of the technique known as muscle reading, or contact mind reading, was the American John Randall Brown (1851-1926).

One way this is done is for the mind reader to hold the wrist of someone from the audience who knows where an object is hidden.

Just by picking up very slight movements from the spectator's arm, the mind reader is able to find out where an object is hidden.

Brown became an expert at this kind of mind reading and performed successfully in America, Cuba, Britain, and Europe.

Animal magic

THE TRICK

Predict what animal will be picked from a long list of animals. Your mental powers will astound the audience. There is also an unexpected visitor in the room...

1 Write the word "Lion" on the cardboard and seal it in the envelope.

2 Place the envelope somewhere in full view.

3 If you don't have a toy lion, you can make one from yellow and orange felt. Copy the shapes below on paper. You can enlarge them on a photocopier if you like.

Preparation

You will need:
- a pen or pencil
- a piece of cardboard
- an envelope
- a toy lion or some felt
- several slips of paper
- a box

4 Pin the paper to the felt and cut around it. Glue the parts together as in the picture. With a marker pen, draw on eyes, nose, mouth, and claws.

5 Hide the toy lion somewhere in the room where you will be performing, for example, behind a curtain or a door.

1

Ask for the names of animals that can be seen in a zoo. As each name is called out, you pretend to write it on one of the slips of paper, without anyone seeing. In fact, you write "Lion" on every slip and then drop it into the box.

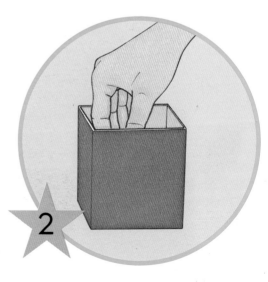

2

Mix up the slips and ask someone to take one out without looking.

18

3

Ask for the name of the chosen animal to be called out. Naturally, it is "Lion"—it can't be anything else. Now have someone open the envelope, read out what is on the card inside, and acknowledge the applause.

Top Tip

• *Asking for animals seen in a zoo almost guarantees that someone will call out "Lion." If you are scared that this might not happen, start off by saying, "I want you to call out the names of animals that you could see in a zoo, such as elephants, tigers, lions, antelopes, and anything you like." This way you can be more certain that someone will call out "Lion."*

• *To make your audience believe that the different animal names they called out are really in the box, you can take one out, read out, "Elephant"—even though it says "Lion"—and put the slip back. Then let someone in the audience take out a slip and read what is on it.*

4

Everyone thinks the trick is over, but you have another surprise up your sleeve! Suddenly pause and say you heard something—a noise from the direction where the toy lion is hidden. Ask someone to go and take a look, and to their surprise they'll find a toy lion!

It's in the stars

THE TRICK

Find the odd one out in a number of cards: without even looking, you can find the one card with a star sign among a group of cards with capital city names.

Preparation

> **You will need:**
> - 10 pieces of cardboard
> - 10 pencils
> - scissors
> - a magazine or newspaper with a horoscope in it
> - an assistant

1 Cut a very fine strip from one end of nine of the cards. The uncut card will be slightly longer than all the others, so you will be able to feel which one it is.

2 Find out what star sign your assistant is, and go through the trick with him so you both know what to do.

1 Hand out the nine short cards to nine different people and give each person a pencil. Ask them to write the name of a capital city on their card.

Hand the long card and a pencil to your friend and ask him to write down the name of a star sign. He should write down his own star sign.

2

Top Tip

You do not, of course, have to stick to cities and star signs. You can have any subject where there is one odd item— comedians and a singer, for example—it is up to you. Keep in mind that the horoscope part of the trick won't work anymore. Find another end to the trick or stop after the part where you show the cards.

20

3

Ask someone to gather up the cards in any order and hand them to you behind your back. You say that you are going to use your mental powers to pick out the star sign card. All you have to do is push all the cards together and you will find it quite easy to pick out the long card.

4

Bring the star sign card forward in one hand and all the other cards in the other hand without looking at them. Ask the audience if the single card is the one with the star sign. This is already quite spectacular, but it gets even better! Now ask your friend to take the magazine and find the page with the horoscope. Ask him to read out his. When he is finished, ask him to tell everyone what the star sign was he just read out. It is of course the one you are holding in your hand!

ROME

Gemini

DID YOU KNOW...

... that the emblem of the world's most famous magic club, The Magic Circle (based in London), consists of the twelve signs of the zodiac?

Divide by four

THE TRICK

Your fantastically powerful brain is able to make any number divisible by 4. Even if that number is ten digits long!

Ask a spectator to write down a very long number, perhaps with as many as ten digits. Take a quick look at it and, no matter what the number is, say, "That is not divisible by 4 but I can make it so."

Preparation

You will need:
- writing paper
- a pen or pencil
- a calculator

Pretend to count on your fingers to figure out how you can make this number divisible by 4.

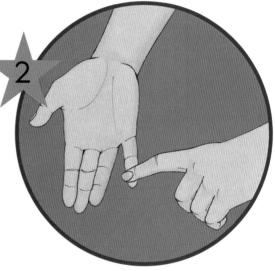

Top Tip

One of the rules of magic is that you should never repeat a trick. This one, however, you can do a couple of times without your audience getting suspicious. You need to add two digits that are themselves divisible by 4, for example: 04, 08, 12, 16, 20, 24 etc. Many of these are so obvious they might give the trick away, so stick with some of the less obvious combinations, such as 52 or 76.

Then add the digits 2 and 8 to the number.

4 Believe it or not the new number is divisible by 4. It will take the spectator quite a while, even with a calculator, to find out that this is true.

Pick a book

THE TRICK

Amaze your friends by talking to...books! Someone picks a book and even though you didn't look, you know which one it was!

Preparation

> You will need:
> • a bookcase containing ten books in a row
> • ten hairs

Place a hair under each one of the books, so that every hair sticks out about an inch.

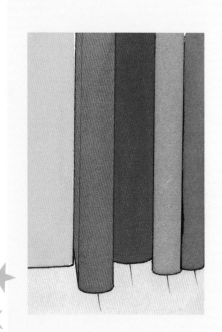

Point to the row of books and say that these are your favorites and that you have a special relationship with them.

Turn your back and ask someone to take out any book, flick through it, and then put it back in exactly the same place.

You now turn to face the audience and go to the bookcase, pretending to be receiving thought waves from the books.

What you are really doing is looking for the hairs you put there earlier. There will be one hair missing and that will show the book that was removed.

Top Tip

• If you want to do this in someone else's house, placing the hairs will be a tricky business. In this case you could take with you a small quantity of salt. When everyone else is out of the room, you put a few grains of salt on the top of each book. By seeing which book has the salt missing, you will know which one has been chosen.

• You can make the trick a bit longer and more interesting by taking out some books and pretending to talk to them. Hold a book to your ear and "listen" to how it tells you which book was removed by the spectator. When you do this, you have to make sure you saw where the hair was missing before you take out any books.

Odd and even

THE TRICK

Your friends will be amazed to see you have X-ray vision! You are able to see which of their closed hands holds an odd and which an even number of small items.

Preparation

You will need:
• seven small objects (stones, marbles, bits of paper, almost anything, providing they can be held in the hands)

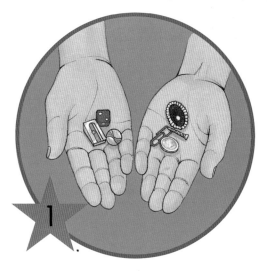

Give a spectator seven objects. Tell him that when your back is turned he should put an even number of them in one hand and an odd number in the other.

Top Tip

This trick works with any odd number of items. It also works with different numbers for the multiplying, providing that the items in the right hand are multiplied by an odd number and the items in the left are multiplied by an even. Using just seven items and multiplying by 5 and 2 keeps everything simple.

$$4 \times 5 = 20$$
$$3 \times 2 = 6$$

Now tell him to multiply the number of items in his right hand by 5. Next he is to multiply the number of items in his left hand by 2.

Ask him to add the two numbers and tell you the result.

$$20 + 6 = 26$$

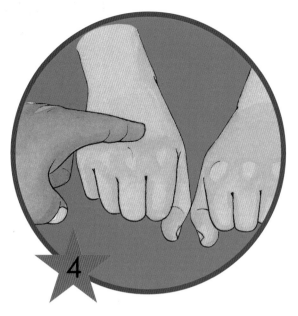

4

You can tell him immediately which hand holds the odd number and which holds the even number. If the result of his calculation is an odd number, then he holds an odd number of objects in his right hand (and an even number in his left). If he reports an even result, he has an even number of items in his right hand (and an odd number in his left).

IT'S MAGIC

Derren Brown

The British performer Derren Brown (b.1971) created a sensation when he starred in his first television series in December 2000.

Like a lot of children, he developed an interest in magic, but it was only later, when he was in college, that he started to take it seriously. He gave up a career in law to become a magician. Gradually, he left behind props and sleight-of-hand to work with psychological techniques. He says, "I have to learn to step inside people's heads. Then I can play." He describes his performance as psychological magic, but to everyone watching, it appears to be true mind reading.

Reds and blacks

THE TRICK

When a spectator deals a shuffled deck of cards, you are able to predict how many more red cards there will be than black!

Preparation

You will need:
- a deck of cards
- some paper
- a pen or pencil

Before you start, take two black cards out of the deck.

❶ When you take out two cards, keep in mind that you don't have a complete deck anymore. This means you may not be able to do other tricks with the same deck.

1 On the piece of paper write, "There will be two more reds than blacks." Do not let anyone see what you have written. Fold the paper up and leave it on the table.

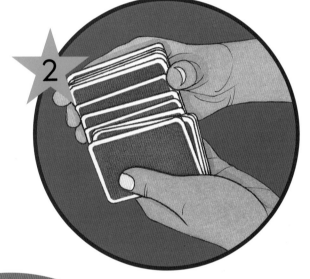

Remove the cards from their case. Ask a spectator to shuffle the cards until he is satisfied that they are well mixed.

DID YOU KNOW...

... that mentalists sometimes use special cards for mental tricks? There are five designs—star, cross, circle, square, and wavy lines. They are often called Zenner cards (after their inventor) or ESP (extrasensory perception) cards.

3

Now ask him to deal the cards, in pairs, face up. If two red cards come together, he has to place them in one pile. If two black ones come together, they go in another pile. If the pair consists of a red and a black card, they are to be placed in a third pile.

Top Tip

To make your audience believe you really have amazing mental powers, you could try this: while the spectator is dealing the cards, pretend you are concentrating very hard as if to influence the way the cards come out. You could ask him to stop for a moment while you touch the deck of cards, as if you were making it do exactly what you want.

4

When all the cards have been dealt, ask the spectator to count the number of cards in the black pile and the number of cards in the red pile.

5

He will have two more reds than he has blacks. Now ask him to open the paper and he will see that this is exactly what you had predicted!

Symbols of magic

THE TRICK

Use your mystical powers to identify the symbol a spectator is thinking of.

Preparation

You will need:
- five blank pieces of cardboard
- pencils or crayons

Memory system

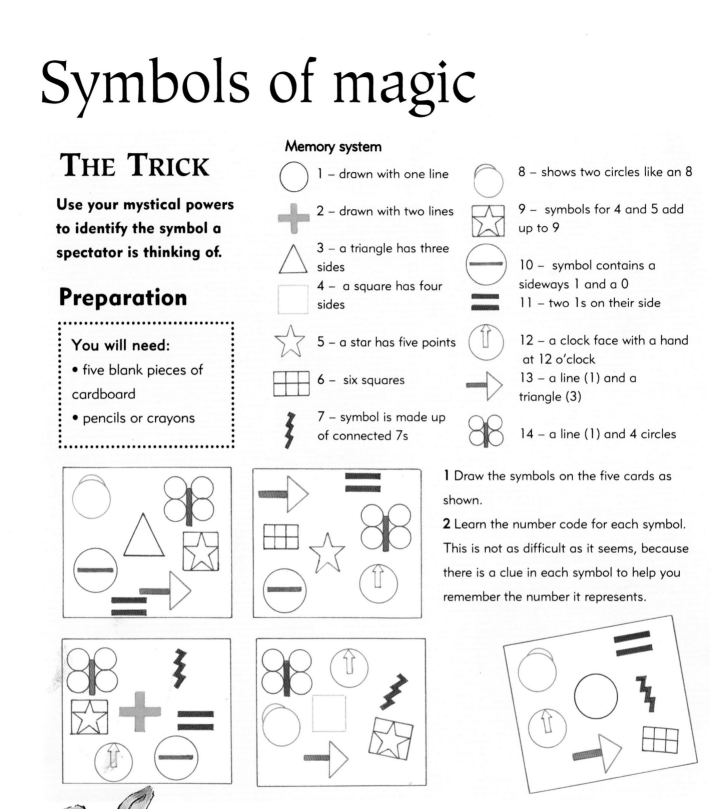

1 – drawn with one line

2 – drawn with two lines

3 – a triangle has three sides

4 – a square has four sides

5 – a star has five points

6 – six squares

7 – symbol is made up of connected 7s

8 – shows two circles like an 8

9 – symbols for 4 and 5 add up to 9

10 – symbol contains a sideways 1 and a 0

11 – two 1s on their side

12 – a clock face with a hand at 12 o'clock

13 – a line (1) and a triangle (3)

14 – a line (1) and 4 circles

1 Draw the symbols on the five cards as shown.

2 Learn the number code for each symbol. This is not as difficult as it seems, because there is a clue in each symbol to help you remember the number it represents.

Top Tip

You can make up your own memory system—this is called mnemonics—for this trick. You just have to make sure the numerical values are the same as the ones used above for the trick still to work.

1

Lay out the five cards on the table and ask someone to think of just one of the symbols on the cards. Let's say she picks the symbol for 10.

Now ask the spectator to take away every card that shows the symbol she is thinking of. Look at the remaining cards and add up the values of the center symbols. In our example, you add up the values for the circle and the square (1 + 4 = 5).

2

15 - 5
=10

3

Subtract the number you get from 15. This will be the numerical value of the symbol the spectator is thinking of. Ask her to "send" the symbol to you mentally. Pretend to "receive" it, and tell her what symbol she was thinking of!

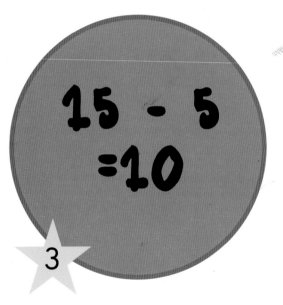

Index

Blaine, David 10
blindfold 7
book test 32
books 14, 15, 24, 25
Brown, Derren 27
Brown, John Randall 17

calculator 13, 22, 23
cities 20

dice 12, 23
dictionary 14
Dunninger, Joseph 15

Germain, Karl 6

hairs 24, 25
horoscope 21

jaw 16, 17

magic wand 14, 15
mentalists 9, 28
mnemonics 30, 32
Morse code 6
muscle reading 17, 32

popsicle sticks 8, 9

Robert-Houdin 23

salt 25
sleight-of-hand 27
star signs 20, 21

temples 16

X-ray vision 26

Zenner cards 28

Glossary of magic words

Book test
Any mind reading trick in which a book is used.

Mnemonics
A technique or system used to improve the memory.

Muscle reading
A method of obtaining information through the subconscious and tiny movements within the nervous system.

Some magicians call it Contact Mind Reading because the performer has to be in contact with the subject.

Prediction
A trick in which the performer appears to have foretold the future.

Telepathy
Communicating using just the power of the mind.

Web sites and clubs

Have you caught the magic bug and want to know more? Here are some Web sites of magic clubs you could join:

• www.magicsam.com
Site of the Society of American Magicians. At age 100, this is the oldest magical society in the world.

• www.magicsym.org
Site of The Society of Young Magicians.

• www.magicyouth.com
Site of the youth program of the International Brotherhood of Magicians.

Magic tricks can be bought from:
• www.internationalmagic.com
• www.merlinswakefield.co.uk
• www.magictricks.com

DISCARD

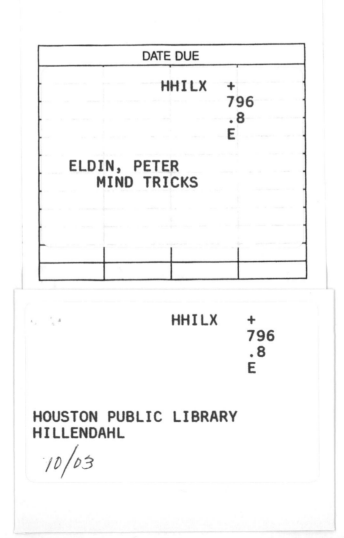